INTERIOROLOGY™

Home Design from Within

How to Create a Living Environment
That Reflects the Inner You

Laurel James

Interior room photography by Matt McCourtney
Interior Design by Laurel Phipps-James
Nature photographs by Michael James
Additional photography by iStock Images
Hand Drawing and equations by Laurel James
Cover design by Beth Noble
Back cover portfolio photo by Lori Sax
Interior portfolio photo by Tamera Williams

The author of this book does not dispense medical advice or prescribe the use of any technique as a form of treatment for physical, emotional, or medical problems without the advice of a physician, either directly or indirectly. The intent of the author is only to offer information of a general nature to help you in your quest for emotional and spiritual well-being. In the event you use any of the information in this book for yourself, which is your constitutional right, the author and the publisher assume no responsibility for your actions.

ISBN: #978-0-692-33399-0

Printed in the United States of America

Acknowledgments

This book is dedicated to my Grandmother Frances Robin Sibley. You are always in my heart and spirit. Being your grand daughter is a blessing and I love you.

To the love of my life Michael James, thank you for your support and for loving me for who I am.

Thank you to my family for encouraging me to follow my heart and do what I love.

Thank you to my friends for the kindness of letting me share and explore my ideas for this book.

A special thanks to; Tamara Williams for the countless hours editing, laughing about "everything", Angela Black for being my home when I didn't have a physical one and for the hours shared imagining what Interiorology could be, Tara Carrington for finding me and sharing an unspoken knowing of home, Audrey Wentworth for being full of tools to share with me, Donna Simmons for being on the journey of home with me and ever full of laughter and light, Kimberly Braun for your friendship and community spirit, Angela Hager for collaborating and being my agent of inspiration and self-expression, Catherine Logan for showing me innovative ways and resources of how to find my natural home inside and out.

My heartfelt thanks to all my Clients whose stories appear in this book and for the ones that do not that still contributed to the process.

Contents

In-te-ri-or-ol-o-gy

(Interior-ology)

-noun

1.　　A self empowering system to help people move through life's transitions in their homes.

2.　　The art of applying physical, emotional, psychological, and spiritual awarenesses in one's living space.

3.　　A guided process through introspection and delightful physical discoveries. It gives one a visual mapping system of what one needs to flourish and thrive in his or her surroundings.

Origin:
2010; See; <u>interior, -home,-psych-</u>, <u>logy</u>

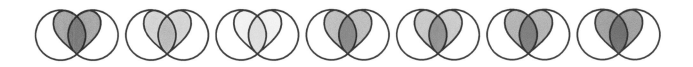

Home—
the center of your interior and exterior world;
it is the keeper of you.
Where you can set up ideas
Like furniture to suit you,
and hang up all your fondest dreams
like pictures on a wall.
You need only be satisfied
with the arrangements of your heart;
to feel loved, joyful, and at peace within.
There is a daily flowing dance
between your inner and outer home,
like two infinite loops
united, moving and changing together.
Your environment
is the reflection of your internal nature.
Illuminate yourself from inside
like a warm table lamp on a cold night.
Breathe, listen, and be present;
relax, let your past go
in the gentle silence of home.

Take a journey with childlike wonder
with your environment as the path;
imagine the home of your dreams, and
move through the front door into that sanctuary.
Tune in to your heart,
knowing you are like a explorer
who can find the multitude
of sounds, colors, tastes, aromas, and textures,
in harmony with what naturally flourishes.
Find your favorite spot;
visualize what you are doing.
Feel nurtured here;
linger in this ambiance.
There is deep enjoyment
knowing what inward awareness brings.
Be inspired in this place that is so lovely.
It belongs to you.

Welcome Home!

Finding Home

My house was empty. Stark, white walls surrounded me like an artist's canvas. I sat on the floor, paint samples spread around me, and I started to cry. I felt stuck; I didn't know where to start with decorating my new home. Here I was, an interior designer for two decades; I had picked thousands of paint colors for hundreds of people, and I couldn't do it for myself! I didn't know where to start or what to choose because my identity was changing in both my professional and my personal life.

For the first time, I was personally experiencing big life-stage changes, like so many of my clients went through when working with me as an interior designer. I was going through a divorce and needed to move into a new living space. At the same time, I was downsizing and relocating my office into this home. With so much change all at once, I felt lost, stuck, unsure of my life's direction and of whom I wanted to become. Why was I, as a professional interior designer, feeling disconnected from what to do for the design of my own home?

I became an interior designer because I wanted to help others feel happier and more connected to their homes. I was privileged to grow up among family members who are artists, architects, builders, and teachers. They all had a sense of their surroundings and how they wanted them to look. My parents, who were divorced, had two separate households, which provided me with the experience of having two bedrooms. I also visited friends' and grandparents' homes often on the weekends, which exposed me to an even wider range of surroundings. From an early age, I loved to learn and to observe people. The experiences of my childhood gave me the opportunity to learn how people lived in many different environments. These homes didn't always feel good to me, and I often wondered as a little girl why my various surroundings didn't always match the unseen feelings I sensed. Even though their homes looked nice on the surface, I sometimes felt serenity was missing from them. The seed was planted: how could I help people make a beautiful space that felt better to them?

As a young adult heading to college, I became interested in social psychology, self-help topics and spatial relationships. Environments and people are still a path of inquisitive journey for me. Even today, I continue to enjoy finding ways to expand my mind and evolve in my life. When I chose to become an interior designer, the choice felt natural. I could combine my interest in understanding people and how they function with the artistry of creating an atmosphere for others.

Early in my career, I started my own interior design firm. It gave me great joy to counsel families and individuals on how to find and enhance their personalities and preferences in order to design their homes. When I saw my clients connected to and living happy lives in their homes, it gave me complete satisfaction. Knowing I could help make their home lives better touched my heart.

One of my favorite parts of the design process was the "getting-to-know-you" stage of design. I used the opportunity to ask many questions of my clients to help design their home. This was the beginnings of Interiorology; bring the unseen feeling out of my client to design their home. Each time I did a project, I created questions about who the person was and what they liked aesthetically. It was like a puzzle about how people felt in their hearts and what they liked to feel in their environments.

The getting-to-know-you stage of design led to the beginning research of Interiorology. I would create systems of all the common personalities and preferences that people needed in their home lives. I loved helping my clients make interior-design decisions based on what was changing for them or what was happening at that moment, instead of focusing on who they had been in the past. The process did include bringing up their treasured memories and furniture pieces from the past but only if they were serving a purpose. Most of putting the puzzle pieces in place was about moving forward, imagining what they wanted and what made them feel good, happy, and peaceful. It was about how I could find and enhance their unique inner qualities and integrate them into their home lives.

Some of my clients feared and resisted divulging their inner selves during the preliminary design stage. They preferred to stay on the surface levels and not open up what was deeper inside.

In turn, I could only work on the surface, and I felt unable to address what they truly wanted and needed in their home environment to feel happy.

On the other hand, those clients who understood themselves and were able to tell me what made them happy benefited most from my design consulting. We could design an integrated home environment for them. We could create places of solace and rejuvenation where they could be themselves. Through my experience with numerous types of clients, I discovered how important and valuable this process was for me. I found out how important it was to represent my client's home in their heart.

Another thing I've noticed about all my clients' home lives is how advancements in technology, communication, and travel are changing our living spaces quicker than ever before. It is hard to keep up with how fast our lives are changing. At the same time, many of us cannot afford to stay in our homes because of financial reasons. Our homes are quickly changing, and our inner spaces are changing too! How can we possibly keep up with the all-too-frequent need to change our homes to match our changing lives? With so many decisions and so much external stimulation, how do we design places to support us when our lives are changing so fast? How could I help others see that we are an extension of our environment and that we move with it? How could I help others create an integrated home to keep up with the fast-moving world?

The day I sat on my floor, trying to pick paint colors for my new home, I was on information overload. There were so many choices to make; I didn't know where to start. I was the one who needed a designer that day! I had to walk away and find solitude and just do nothing for a moment. I needed the space to remember how I had guided many of my clients to find their "inner compass" of what home was to them. Just as in the preliminary design stages I had worked through with my clients, I now needed to ask myself the same questions. I had to remember my inner self. I became aware that my home and I are in a relationship, moving through life together. During my self-discovery, I learned that I had to feel my way through the process, so that my home would reflect my authentic self. Today my home is integrated with who I am—and who I am becoming— and my journey of self-discovery was an important piece of that puzzle.

As I remembered how to design my living space, something inside me was emerging. I wanted to create a map for others to use at any time in their life, to design their own homes to feel harmonious and happy. With so many fast changes in our home lives, I wanted others to have access to my intuitively guided system. Therefore, I wrote this book as a gift, to be like a trusted companion to turn to when they are alone, cannot afford a designer, or don't know how to move forward with their home.

Introduction

At the heart of your home life is the inner you. All the parts of what you have experienced, where you are now, and where you want to go in the future are inside of you. This book has the keys that can unlock the front door of your inner home and heart, to find the treasures you need to design your living space. Come with me on a journey as we discover Interiorology.

You are like a snowflake that is different from all others. You have unique abilities, talents, emotions, opinions, ideas, and beliefs. Regardless of our culture, our age, or where we live, we all need a physical shelter, a home to which we return for rest and rejuvenation. We desire a place of grounding, centering, and peace. We also need to feel happy, loved, and supported in our homes. Ask yourself: who lives in the heart of your home?

In this book, I will show you a new method of finding your home in an ever-changing world. It will serve as an introduction to the process I call Interiorology. I created this system by combining more than twenty years of hands-on experience as an interior designer, doing private Interiorology sessions, and interactive workshops and retreats. I've gathered all the information and questions I shared with my clients, and I'm introducing it to you in this book, so you can begin the journey of exploring and experiencing your authentic self. This overview of the process will provide insights into your inner and outer home. You will begin to discover that your inner self and your surroundings are in a continuous dance together.

We all have many life passages as we walk through life. Regardless of age or financial circumstances, my clients are going through some type of life change. Sometimes we are forced to change or to start over in our homes or in our lives. Other times we are excited and looking forward to a new home or a new life stage. No matter where you are, stop for a moment and take a deep breath. This is the starting point of the Interiorology process and the first chapter. When things are unclear in life, we need that space to stop and clear up the clutter of life and just breathe. We need quiet each day, to collect our thoughts, to let things go, to reflect and hear our inner voice. Like the foundation of a house that supports walls and a roof, a period of silence brings us strength to uphold our lives.

In chapter two, we will explore the kinds of patterns you learned in your formative years. How did you feel in your childhood home? What things did you love as a child? For me, it was growing up in a home by the water—a sensation that was missing when I moved into my new home. This new home was the first place I had lived that was not directly on a body of water. Therefore, when it came time to pick paint colors and finishes, I incorporated aqua colors to remind me of the water. I even put a soothing fountain in the center of my home, giving me the feeling of expansiveness. Having physical things in my space that represented what I loved from my childhood home made me feel creative in my living space. The simple act of bringing in meaningful elements from my past helped me feel personally and uniquely connected to my home. We will playfully explore different prints and patterns, inviting you to draw inspiration from things you liked in childhood.

I want to help you move past any place you may feel stuck or off balance. I felt this way while going through changes in my personal and professional spaces. I realized my heart and inner home had become overgrown with thorns and thickets of ideas, fears, defenses, prejudices, and repressions. Pieces of me had lain dormant because so many things had grown up around me to create walls and defenses.

In the third chapter, we will look at where you are at today, to help you become aware of where you want to go tomorrow. Just as trees lose their leaves, so things naturally change in our homes. Remember that the roots of the tree are very much alive, just as you are, inside. Even if the limbs of the tree are cut or are going through a harsh winter, they will still grow back, nurtured by rain and the warmth of spring. See these life changes as part of your life's ceremonies. They give you the potential and possibilities for growth; knowing this today can give you a perspective for the home you need for tomorrow!

The fourth chapter is the heart of the book. It talks about how living in harmony in your home can come from connecting your inner self and your home with nature. Just as a flower needs the right environment to bloom, so we need the right home in which to grow and thrive. When I bring elements I love from nature into my home, it looks and feels connected to the natural world. I feel more connected, like I did when visiting my grandparents' farm when I was growing up. Their home had a natural simplicity to the elements inside that reflected what was in the outside environment. Everything from the stone fireplace to the wood floor was a mirror of the landscape surrounding them. When we feel a connection with nature and integrate those elements into our homes, we create an environment in which we grow and flourish.

In the fifth chapter, we will consider how you feel, live, and function in your home which will lead you to creating a space that is you. My grandparents' home was an ideal example of self expression.   My grandmother was an artist and a poet, and my grandfather was a builder. Every wall was adorned with artwork by Grandma and custom-made frames by Grandpa. Their farm home was an authentic expression that illuminated who they were and how they lived. Everyone has a different lifestyle, set of activities, culture, and sense of space, and our lives are all full of different colors, personalities, and preferences. Our homes are our vital places of self-expression. I invite you to follow your feelings to find your home design.

In chapter six, we will imagine how you want to feel in your home. Placing your thoughts on what you want and what you love leads you to an inner and outer home that supports your dreams. Listen to your heart and your "inner knower"—that is the inner space at the center of you. Intentional placement of objects helps reflect who you are and what you want to manifest in the future. It can help you feel optimistic and reminds you of what is important in your heart and home.

Chapter seven offers a time for reflection. All this introspection may seem selfish and self-centered, especially if you are trying to connect with others in your home, but finding your way home first is the biggest service you can give to others. Being at home in the world means knowing yourself first. That place of unity in your heart and home is found when you get clear on who you are. There will be an expansion of room for others in your heart and your life when you are grounded, curious, aware, integrated, expressive, and mindful within yourself. It is my hope that this process and this book will help you find your way home.

Prescriptions

At the end of each chapter of this book is an Interior Prescription. This is your time to play, practice, and learn one thing about yourself and one thing about how to change your home, based on each chapter's concept. It's okay to discover what is not right, what no longer works, and what is incompatible first, in order to get to what is right for you and your home. Remember, "When one door closes, another one opens." I know that uncertainties and changes usually do not feel like opportunities while they are happening. In retrospect, I realized my difficult experiences were just what I needed to move forward into a home that reflected who I am.

One way to approach this book is by focusing on one chapter at a time. It is your own personal journey, so taking a day, a week or a month is your decision. Another approach I suggest is reading over the entire book and then going back and doing the chapter prescriptions you feel you need, ones you find pertinent at the time. You and your home will change again and again, so you might want to keep your discoveries in a journal. Return to this book as often as you need to, as your life and circumstances change. Interiorology is a tried-and-true process, meant to be used in the ever-changing times of our lives.

Of course, designing our home lives may involve compromise with our partners, families, or roommates. Respect the differences and focus on what you have in common. This is the key: look for all the similarities and positive things that each person contributes to the home life. What are the endearing qualities of the loved ones in your home? What are the common values? Finding the positive aspects of my clients and couples was the cornerstone to the success of any type of design project.

Walk down this path with me. Play with childlike curiosity. Travel to your inner world. Let the discovery of your inner music, joys, and loves begin your transformation. Give yourself the gift of experiencing your unique interior design. Your inner self is a priceless key to your authentic self and home.

The caterpillar instinctively knows and trusts that the butterfly is within. You may be surprised by what you find inside yourself. Experiment with my suggestions, and choose what works for you at the time. Trust your "inner knower" to tell you what is right for you. This is your opportunity to take a journey into yourself and connect with your home. I hope this book will enhance your life by helping you understand the beauty and fullness your home within has to offer. Explore your way through this book with curiosity, and dream of how you would like your home, your heart, and your life to be. Let Interiorology guide you to find your way home. In my heart, I am right there with you. I can't wait to show you what you can do!

You + Heart = Home

What is in your heart?

Chapter 1

Clearing Space

"A tower nine stories high starts with one brick
A journey of a thousand miles begins with a single step."
—Tao Te Ching, Sixty-fourth Verse

In our world, which is forever rotating, moving, and changing, it is important to find a foundation to help us feel grounded. Clearing our inner and outer space will help us achieve stability and order in our home life. Cleaning up from the inside of ourselves to the outside of our environment makes us feel more settled in our homes. Do you feel like you have some breathing room every day, to stop and take a moment to collect your thoughts? Do you have spaces in your home that are clear of clutter, where you can unwind and just be?

We all want a physical place where we can be at ease and be ourselves. Why not start looking at your inner home? It is always there for you. Clearing your inner space helps create a stable foundation upon which to build. You may be going through changes, growing or collecting clutter; but at the beginning of creating a physical home is something you already are: you! It is not a material thing that you possess; you just are. No one can take away your inner home; it is your being, your home within, and it is always there for you. A fundamental principle of Interiorology is clearing away the clutter within. Listen to your heart. Follow your feelings to find your way home, one step at a time from the inside out.

We all experience clutter in our home lives, feeling this external clutter with all our senses: smell, taste, sight, hearing, and touch. We all know the kind of disorder that comes from too many things accumulating in one place or another. These are the things that have been sitting around and taking up space for days, weeks, or even years. Many of them we have been holding on to unnecessarily or we plan to get rid of someday. We may not be aware of the clutter this is causing in our daily home lives, but our senses are taking it all in just the same.

Do you have any junk piles in your house? Be honest. Even being a designer for more than twenty years, I have junk! In fact, I even designed my home with designated places for junk. When I ordered my kitchen sink, I intentionally ordered the biggest, deepest sink available, so that when I placed all of my dirty dishes down in it, they would not be visible to others.

When we turn our computers on to start our workday, we have to deal with junk e-mails. This visual clutter is disturbing! It's hard to focus on the task of working when we have a hundred e-mails in our mailbox that arrived since the last time we logged on.

Just as our computers freeze and stop working when they have been overloaded with

too much information, our minds and bodies can also get overloaded with too much stuff in our living spaces. These cluttered and disorganized areas disturb our inner being every time we walk by them or go near them. We may only catch this junk out of the corner of our eyes, but we are subconsciously cluttering our minds by being around it.

I once had a client who had a home full of sonic clutter. The challenge was, she needed a quiet space in which to unwind, but there was a television or a computer on in every room of her house. Her husband liked to have the TV on most of the time when he was home, and her two children also liked having their shows on in an adjacent open room. Too much sonic clutter was happening at once in their household. We settled the noise down by having the family agree not to have more than one TV on in the main open areas at a time. I suggested low-volume headphones for those using a computer that shared a room with a TV. We also immediately pulled an existing chair and ottoman into her bedroom, providing a much-needed space where she could close the door and silence the noise clutter. There she could take a moment to breathe, clear her thoughts, and be at peace.

The first part of the Interiorology prescription is to stop and take breathing time for yourself each day. Breathing is the foundation of our dwelling place. Take several deep breaths, and let the busy details of your lives go. Relax into your environment. Have no agenda for this moment in time. Sit, listen, and feel the quiet. If thoughts are running through your mind, that's okay. Just breathe; it will help to clean and clear your mind.

When I host any Interiorology session, workshop, or retreat, I always start with meditation. It grounds us, clears our thoughts, and opens our minds and hearts to things we would like to imagine for our home life. Making time to stop and just be is the first step. It gives you time to clear your mind, hear the essence of your inner self, and focus on what you want.

Think of clearing your mind as a lifestyle. Begin going to the "Peaceful Mind Gym" at a specific time for a certain number of times each week. We go to gyms to work out, get exercise, and get healthier. Why not take time for your mind to relax and clear the clutter? Take time to feel your breath. Sweep through all of your thoughts, good and bad, and let the clutter go. Having the free space in your mind clears the way for you to listen to your heart and hear what you want and need in your environment. The key is finding the quiet space in your physical home. You may also need to set boundaries for your family, asking them not to disturb you for a set amount of time. If you feel more comfortable moving around, take a quiet walk outside to find a space and time just for you. Ten to twenty minutes once a day is a good goal. Starting with ten minutes and working your way up is a realistic way to find your comfort level. Just like going to the gym, you don't want to overdo it on the first day. Trust yourself, and you will know what feels right for you.

When we pay attention to the act of breathing, we permit ourselves access to our minds and hearts, allowing certainty and clarity to enter our experiences. To achieve a peaceful home, consider this analogy to airplane safety instructions: "Put your oxygen mask on first before assisting others." If we know who we are in our inner worlds, it will be clearer how we want our outer surroundings to support us.

The second part of this Interiorology prescription involves clearing one space in your home that feels cluttered. Just take one area that is really distracting you. Take a small step in clearing the path toward simplicity and order. Maybe you have a favorite chair or table that is piled high with

magazines that you are going to read "one day." Perhaps your desk area has stacks of papers and books of things you want to do, but the chaos is so overwhelming that you don't know where to start. An example in my own home is my drop-off area, the place where I come in, throw my purse, mail, receipts, change, things to return, and things I am going to fix … one day. You know the place. We all have this area somewhere in our homes. I call this the "drop-off and launching area." It is usually somewhere near an entrance to your home. Often it is a desk, a kitchen spot, a place near the garage entrance, or sometimes even in your bedroom. If you are feeling overwhelmed in this area, it is a great place to start to clear the clutter!

My drop-off and launching area is tucked away in a corner on my kitchen counter. When the junk begins to stack up, I put the mail and receipts away in the correct files. Then I weed through the recyclables and the things to give or throw away. The rest of the stuff to do "someday" slides right into my junk drawer. This gets these objects off the counter, and I know the drawer can only hold so much before I have to clean it out. In fact, I have a designated drawer for everyone in the family! This process keeps the kitchen counter clean. When anyone asks me is the location of their "fill-in-the-blank," the response is easy: "Check your drawer." Keeping the kitchen counter clean is important, because the kitchen is the main social hub of the home. Having clear space there supports your friends, family, and yourself in your home.

Like the fresh smell of a summer shower, a clear space and a few minutes of quiet time can change our mood in an instant. Let go of the clutter in your mind and clear away the things in your home that no longer serve you. The foundation of what you want in the future can begin when you clean up your internal home. The physical distractions in your home are often not as disturbing when your mind is clear. Creating breathing room in both your inner and outer place brings you grounding and clarity for the journey to your true home.

Clearing Space

You + Clearing = Home

INTERIOROLOGY™

Prescription

Clearing Space

For: *You*   **Date:** _____

IP

Stop and take some breathing room for yourself each day.

Notes _____
_____
_____
_____

Side Effects:

This may cause you to feel clear in your home.

INTERIOROLOGY™

Prescription

Clearing Space

For: *Home*   **Date:** _____

IP

Clear one space in your home that you feel is cluttered.

Notes _____
_____
_____
_____

Side Effects:

This may cause your home to be orderly for you.

Chapter 2

Prints and Patterns

"The things which the child loves remain in the domain of the heart until old age."
—Kahlil Gibran

Getting back to your inner child is the next step to finding your authentic home. It is about what you loved doing and remembering the things you treasured as a child. When you see a certain print or patterned fabric, does it make you think of your childhood home? Does the smell of something cooking remind you of those times? Have you ever made a meal you enjoyed from your childhood?

Your childhood homes and family experiences can influence how you live and how you design your home. Your sense memories affect how you feel about your environment. Being aware of the things that were bitter or sweet to you in your childhood home helps you find the hidden essence of you and what you need in your living space today. You started creating and becoming who you are during the formative years of childhood. If you have a clear idea of where you started, it will help you understand who you are now and who you want to be in the future.

When we look at the history of our homes in an Interiorology session, I ask questions that explore how we form our separate identities from our parents. One way we do this is by building homes within homes. Some examples of this are: forts with pillows and blankets, a quiet space under furniture or in a favorite closet or cabinet. We discover not only those marvelous little spaces but also what it was like being by ourselves. Using our imagination and creativity, we discover who we are and what we love.

For example, when I asked a male client where his secret space was, he reflected on the fact that he did not have a place of his own because he shared a bedroom with his brother. However, he did have the bottom bunk bed, and when he was lying in it and looking up, he was in the perfect spot that no one knew about. He distinctly remembered liking that his brother and parents did not know it was there. Taping pictures of motorcycles, mountains, beaches, and trucks, travel articles, and other "boy stuff" to the bottom of the upper bunk was his favorite secret pastime. He went to sleep staring at these things he loved and wanted. Until we explored memories of his childhood, he had forgotten that he had created this collage. Without knowing it, he was forming his own identity and dreams of who he would become. I pointed out to him that he had a lot of those things in his real life today. He has a motorcycle and travels between the mountains and the beach. It was delightful to see his face as he contemplated what he had manifested.

When exploring your childhood, past fears, grief, guilt, and pain may come up. It is never too late to create your home, even if you did not have it under your first roof! Be gentle and compassionate with yourself. Forgive yourself and your loved ones. Dwell on your positive, childlike joys and dreams so that you can create your home from within for today.

By following your heart, you can find what you want for your home. As children, we are free to discover and imagine the world; we explore our environment using our senses as well as through trial and error. When we started to walk, we fell and got back up. When we touched something too hot, we learned to not touch it. Through all the trails and errors, time and experience, we formed memories and patterns. Sometimes we lost the taste for what interested us and what we enjoyed from our formative learning years.

As adults, we need to allow ourselves the freedom to explore the wonderment of life. What activities did you enjoy as a child? What motivated you? What did you like to learn about?

The first part of the prescription is to do something every day that you loved as a child. Bring out the child within you. For example, dance in your living room, sing in the shower, take a bubble bath, or draw to your heart's content. (Stick figures and color are allowed!) With childlike curiosity, look for what made you happy as a child, and carry those things into your adult life.

One of my fondest memories of childhood was being at the dinner table with my brothers, sister, stepmom, and dad. Even the family dog and cat were around the table. I wanted to create happy, memorable times like those from my childhood, repeating the pattern by having a second family myself. Dinnertime at my house today is a time to share our day, eat healthy food, and have a happy, loving space together, as in some of my childhood memories.

The second part of the prescription is to take a look around your home with a child's eye, as if you are seeing your space for the first time. What did you like about your childhood home? Do you see any repeated patterns now? Do you have similar decorating styles and colors, or is your taste completely opposite? Walk through each room, and discover what fills you with delight. Pick your favorite artifact or furniture piece in each room. Like picking your most prized piece of candy out of a Jar full, pick that one thing you love that satisfies your sweet tooth in each space.

Choose the good memories and physical treasures from your childhood home that make you feel fulfilled. Nurture your child within. Remember the things you loved as a child. Doing this will create a more playful, nourishing, and productive home that feeds your heart.

1. Fold Square paper in half.

2. Cut out half of heart shape.

3. Open for Complete heart.

Making Prints and Patterns

You + Child-like Essence = Home

INTERIOROLOGY™

Prescription

Prints and Patterns

For: *You*   **Date:** _____

IP

Once daily do something you loved as a child.

Notes _____
_____
_____
_____

Side Effects:

This may cause you to feel creative in your home.

INTERIOROLOGY™

Prescription

Prints and Patterns

For: *Home* **Date:** _____

IP

Walk through each room in your home with child like curiosity.

What is one thing in each room that makes you feel happy like a child?

Notes _____

_____

_____

_____

Side Effects:

This may cause your home to be personalized for you.

Chapter 3

Perspectives

"Noticing is the way to beauty."
—Jaye Martin, international yoga teacher

Seeing where your home life is off balance today can create a better home for you tomorrow. Noticing where you are in your life at this moment, good or bad, is key. Consider whether or not your surroundings are aligned with where you want to go. Being aware of how you are feeling and viewing things from the perspective of what works and what does not can help move you in a positive direction. In order to move forward, there are many different directions from which to view your life. What is going on in your home, from your point of view? Are you going through any changes in your home life? Does your home feel like the person you see yourself becoming?

An interior designer's job, among other things, is to protect and enhance the health, safety, and welfare (physical, mental, and social well-being) of the public's environment. To meet these requirements, I take into account the whole person and the family, so I am designing authentically for them. The word "health" comes from the Old English root word for "whole." Looking at the whole of your life and your surroundings provides a direction for designing the home you want. When I am hired as an interior designer or Interiorologist, I find that my clients are often going through some sort of life-stage change and need help making transitions in their physical homes. Everyone goes through many stages in life. Some examples include: first homes, room additions for the birth of a child, job relocations, health challenges, divorces, retirements, and deaths. When we experience transitions, our homes also need to change in order to support us and help us thrive.

In addition to the many potential life changes, there are also individual aspects within your home life. I call these "life angles." Some examples of these are career (life journey), health (well-being), creativity (expression), wealth, partnerships (romance), family, and friendships. These different life angles relate to how we feel about, live in, and design our physical home. They are the perspectives we see in our home lives that reflect who we are and where we want to go.

For example, in a past Interiorology workshop, we looked at what kind of overall life stage was happening in our lives and what life angles were feeling out of sorts. I asked the participants to mentally walk through each room of their home and see if there were any clues as to what might be off balance. One of the participants contemplated the question and realized that she was in the middle of a major life change. Her husband was moving his business into their house while they still had young children sharing their home. This major life change necessitated a larger home. She also realized that one life angle—specifically her romance angle—was feeling stuck. When she imagined walking through her current house, she described piles of leftover office equipment, including a paper shredder in their master bedroom! Her observation led to an awareness that gave her the direction she needed to get her romance angle back into alignment.

A few months later, I visited her new home, and with pride and joy she showed me her master suite. She had moved the things that belonged in an office into a separate space. Now her husband had the perfect home office for his new business. With the office equipment in a new location, she was inspired to create a romance box, used to hold love letters between her and her husband. She also designated a special area in the room to play music and enjoy private moments together. Being aware of how she felt and what was happening at that moment gave her direction on how to align with her home. Merely moving a few things created a spark that lit a fire of ideas to incorporate in designing their new home. This simple process made her life easier and happier than she had imagined.

The Interiorology prescription for this chapter is to look at one life angle that needs attention in your home life today. First, take a moment for yourself and notice how you are feeling. Are you going through any major life-stage changes? Are you perhaps feeling unhappy in a particular angle of your life? If you are feeling overwhelmed in many areas, just choose one of your needs that feels the most important at the moment. Feel from your heart. What is one thing that may help to spark your ideas and set you in a good direction?

Next, take the life angle that you want to address, and walk through your home. This is the next part of the prescription. What feels out of place for you? Do you see any clues about what you want or need in your home? Stay open to what you can do to improve this life angle.

For example, your body may feel out of sorts. Maybe you have not been exercising lately, and you are low on energy. Your health life angle needs your attention. As you walk through your home, you may see stacks of clothes hanging over your treadmill in a bedroom. There is a clue! Your home is showing you what you need to change, so you can improve your health life angle.

Accept and appreciate where you are today. Be willing to look at what may need to change in your life and your home at this moment. Noticing what needs changing helps you plant the seeds of optimism, growth, and joy for your future. Using your heart, be aware of where you are today and how you are feeling. Just as a compass helps you find your way, your heart will lead you to your true home.

Perspectives

You + Today = Home

INTERIOROLOGY™

Prescription

Perspectives

For: *You*   **Date:** _____

IP

What is one life angle in your environment today that feels like it needs attention?

Notes _____
_____
_____
_____

Side Effects:

This may cause you to feel guided in your home.

INTERIOROLOGY™

Prescription

Perspectives

For: *Home*   **Date:** _____

IP

Walk through your surroundings with your life angle in mind. Is your home leaving you any clues of the direction you want or need for tomorrow?

Notes _____
_____
_____
_____

Side Effects:

This may cause your home to be directive for you.

Chapter 4

Natural Elements

"Live in the sunshine, swim the sea, and drink the wild air".
—Ralph Waldo Emerson

When we know what we love from nature and bring those elements inside our hearts and homes, we access what we need to design a home that will flourish and grow. Have you ever felt poorly and wanted to go home, wrapped yourself in a soft blanket to rejuvenate, and felt better in the comfort of your living space?

When we bring nature into our homes, it encourages us to feel sensory richness: from the flowers we breathe, spices we taste, colors we see, textures we touch, and sounds we hear. Our bodies integrate with the natural world around us. Just as the sun warms our skin on a cold day, connecting with nature brings us peace between our physical senses and our mental self. When we join together with nature in our homes, we root ourselves to the earth that sustains us. Nature has fresh air, cleansing rains, and soothing sunshine. It helps us maintain our physical, mental, and emotional selves by providing all the elements we need to thrive.

Bringing nature into our space can invite us past the busyness of our minds and cultivate the feeling in our hearts. It is natural to want to feel happy and not suffer. Many studies have shown that when we feel we are part of nature, we feel better. When we are disconnected and cut off from our natural environment, we develop a false sense of self. The more time we spend in nature, the more positive our image of self becomes.

Have you ever felt the need to go outside and get some fresh air and clear your thoughts?

Does taking a walk on the beach and listening to the sound of the waves soothe you? Or do you prefer the feeling of being in a forest or garden? Our bodies adapt and connect to nature by being in nature; it heals, comforts, and helps us feel more expansive inside. We share the elements with the natural earth; we are a part of it. We heal and are alive like it is. Embracing the natural things from the earth soothes, stimulates, and fills an inherent need within us.

A young family, clients of mine, wanted to create a fun, colorful vacation home in Florida. Most of their time was spent in the Northeast, where it was cold and cloudy. So when we began designing their place, they knew that they wanted to bring the feeling of the tropics inside. Choosing refreshing aqua colors of the water and warm burnt oranges of the sunsets gave them a natural feeling that was perfect for them. By bringing into their environment the natural elements of the tropical sunsets and clear waters that they loved, they were able to feel connected to their home.

The first part of the prescription is to spend time being outdoors and discovering what you love in nature. Selecting an area outside in which to eat fresh, natural foods can revitalize your mind and body. No chairs or table outdoors? Take a blanket and have a picnic! If it is too hot or too cold or it's raining, find a place

near a window, and bring live plants inside.

Whenever I begin an interior design project or Interiorology session, I find it essential to get to know each client. Each person comes to the session with his or her own unique personality traits and preferences. The key to any type of home project is for clients to open up and let me know what they want and feel. Getting into nature will help you find and connect with yourself and what you truly want in a home.

Just like unconditional love, nature is always with you. You can count on the sun rising every day, the moon becoming full once a month, and the stars being there, whether you can see them or not. Become aware of what you love and how things in nature affect you. When you are in nature, notice what touches your heart and what patterns, textures, and shapes you love.

The next part of the Prescription is bringing nature inside your living space. Bring in the natural elements you love, to fill up your senses and create your interior landscape. Consider one natural thing for each of your five senses that can bring you comfort and joy in your living space. For example, what colors do you like to look at in nature? Bring those colors in with paints, accent pillows, or flowering plants. Does a soft blanket feel appealing to your touch? Does the cool tile feel good on your bare feet? Does a crackling fireplace, water fountain, or wind chimes sound good to you in your living space? You naturally live with nature. You breathe air, bathe in water, and eat from the Earth. You are an extension of your environment. Being aware of what you love from nature and incorporating elements in your home will guide you to a connected feeling in your heart.

Unconditional love and support come from within our hearts and homes. Like the roots of a tree, our homes can nourish and encourage us to grow to limitless possibilities when we bring in what we love from nature. No matter how far we branch out or have to bend with the wind, nature and our interior home are always there for us. Keep nature in your heart and your living space, so you can flourish from the inside out!

Natural Elements

You + Nature = Home

INTERIOROLOGY™

Prescription

Natural Elements

For: *You*　　　　　　　　**Date:** _____

IP

Once a day get into nature to connect with yourself.

Notes _____
_____
_____
_____

Side Effects:

This may cause you to feel connected in your home.

INTERIOROLOGY™

Prescription

Natural Elements

For: *Home*　　　　　　**Date:**_____

IP

Bring elements of nature you love into your home.

Notes _____
_____
_____
_____

Side Effects:

This may cause your home to be integrated with you.

Chapter 5

Form Follows Feeling

"Music is what life sounds like"
—Eric Olson

Living is like music, and home is the instrument. What we feel and do in our lives guides us to be in tune with the way we need to design our homes. Does your life make you feel like you have room to play? Is there something you would like to explore and learn about? Consider arranging one place in your home where you can express yourself.

Just as humans have unique roles and personalities, each home has different functions and styles. Mammals can vary, from giraffes on land to dolphins in the water; human habitations can be just as different. If a yoga instructor were to see a picture of a formal, decorated, cozy room with no floor space for stretching or moving, it may not appeal to him or her because of this person's particular lifestyle. This yogi's lifestyle needs more expansive space for movement and activities. On the other hand, if a librarian who loves reading sees the same picture of this smaller room, it may be more in tune with what he or she would want in a living space, because it is a more intimate and focused atmosphere.

We all relate and function differently in our environment based on our feelings, preferences, roles, and lifestyles. Before starting an Interiorology session or interior design project, the client and I create a plan. I need to know what feelings and needs my clients have, how they currently live, and their desires for the future. When planning the interior of the physical home, each room should amplify how that family feels and lives. There is a rhythm of feelings, functions, and forms, in it that is harmonious with the people who live there. We all want the feelings of being satisfied, rested, connected, invigorated, and happy. We also need to consider function within our lifestyle and the

roles we play. We eat, sleep, socialize, and learn in different ways. Our surroundings have kitchens, bedrooms, living rooms, dens, and playrooms that help us feel and function in ways that are unique to us. Our homes and lives are on a continuous rhythmic flow together, moving to the beat of what we feel, what we do, and how our spaces function.

At times, the rhythms of life change, and we feel the need to re-arrange our homes to accommodate our growth. One of my clients and her family's priorities and lifestyle were evolving, and they wanted to stay in their existing home. The children were becoming teenagers, and their needs were changing. The mother was still very active in their lives, yet she was growing a business. This created a need for more space for storage and work areas than she currently had. She was also finding it increasingly hard to find time and space for her and her husband. This growth left no space for the mother to have much-needed time for herself. We needed to design a new space plan for the things she needed to do, so she could be in sync with her physical space.

We took a walk around her house to find more space for her expanding business. At the time, she had a work desk in the living room and one in her kitchen that were primarily for her business. We needed to find a separate space that would help distinguish her work area from her personal home life. We found her guest bedroom

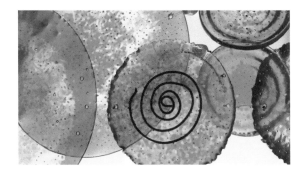

hardly being used, so we decided to convert it into her office. We arranged tables, filing systems, and everything she needed in this room so that she could close the door and walk away from work, thereby allowing her to focus on the family "after hours."

After looking around the house, I also identified something that the mother enjoyed doing for herself: she loved to look through body, mind, and spirit wellness magazines. She had collected them in stacks that she wanted to read and enjoy one day but could never get around to it. First we weeded through the ones she wanted to keep. Then we moved two comfy chairs into the master bedroom and brought in a basket to hold the treasured magazines to read in the newly established space. As we moved objects around in the master bedroom, a variety of emotions and feelings emerged as she began to plan out how she wanted it to feel—simple and spa-like. She could see a space being formed for not only herself when she needed to relax, but a second space for her husband, having two chairs in the room. Delightfully, the changes resulted in a peaceful and welcoming space not only for herself but also a much-needed space for couple time.

Discussing how the client felt about her changing family helped us to know how and where to place her furniture. The result created a harmonious space that supported the family's well-being and enhanced their new rhythm while giving them a way to stay in their existing home.

The first part of the prescription is "function follows feeling." How do you feel within your heart? What does your heart and mind want to express? The word "emotion" contains the word "motion" within it. Our feelings are meant to move us and inspire our home lives. When we are able to move and express our feelings, we can plan what we need and want for our living spaces. Make room in your life for self-expression. Choose one thing that inspires you to learn, grow, and enjoy.

Consider making time during the week to do so. Examples of this could include reading, writing, taking an online class, cooking, painting, learning a musical instrument, or photography. When there is a plan to have free space set aside, creativity can come out and play.

The second part of the prescription is for your living space. Forms follow functions. How do you want or need to function in your environment while doing this activity? How can it be accomplished in your space? Where can you find a spot to accomplish it? Start by finding the place in your home. Examples can be an end table, a chair, a desk, a physical room, a garage space, or outside areas. Walk around your home and consider spaces and furniture that may not be utilized very often and how they could be used for your activity. Finding an area helps remind you to do the thing you love. You are also more likely to follow your passion when there is an organized space in which to do it.

You are the composer of your life. Find the rhythm between you and your home. Start with what moves you emotionally and what feels good to do in your home. Think of how you and your space want to function and flow during your activity. Plan to give yourself time and space to explore and play. The result brings with it a sense of order and peace; you're taking action on the things you want to do within your surroundings. When you plan space in your life to do one thing you enjoy, you are free to be at home within.

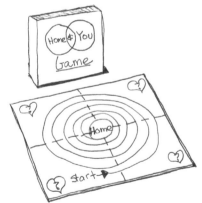

Form Follows Feeling

You + Feeling = Home

INTERIOROLOGY™

Prescription

Form Follows Feeling

For: *You*　　　　　**Date:** _____

IP

Create space in your life to do one thing you enjoy doing on a weekly basis.

Notes _____
_____
_____
_____

Side Effects:

This may cause you to feel expressive in your home.

INTERIOROLOGY™

Prescription

Form Follows Feeling

For: *Home*   **Date:** _____

IP

Plan a place in your home to do this activity.

Notes _____

_____

_____

_____

Side Effects:

This may cause your home to be functional for you.

Chapter 6

Décor

"A house is built of walls and beams. A home is built with love and dreams"
—unknown

Your dreams and feelings are found at the center of you. Visualize how you want to feel and then place your décor in your living space to create your true home. When I am creating an interior design project for a client, we spend the first stage of design getting a clear picture of what the client wants. Next we develop a purposeful design according to the client's personal values, dreams, and desires. Knowing all of this, I am able to help the client focus on the aesthetics and choose furniture and decorations that can support them in their home life. Intentional placement is a timeless way to design and decorate that never goes out of style. How do you need to feel to be "at home"? What do you want your home to reflect about you? What does your dream home look like?

No matter what culture we live in, the décor in our homes sets the stage and plays a role in our lives. Our values, personalities, and spiritual beliefs share the same space with our items, artifacts, and knick-knacks. All together, they provide an external expression of our personalities and styles. Intentional placement is an exterior symbol of our true selves and our hopes and dreams.

Sometimes if we are not conscious of our placement in our homes, we can send the wrong signal. For instance, I had been living in my new home for a year after being divorced, and I realized that I had a single chair placed in almost every room in my house. As I walked through my house, I became mindful of how I had been unconsciously giving off a signal that I just wanted to be left alone. With one chair and no seating for visitors and loved ones, I had been unintentionally sending a signal that I did not want company! At that moment, I became aware of what I wanted with a clear

intention: I wanted to share my life with positive friends. I needed my home to be welcoming and to reflect my core values of love and joy.

Therefore, with intention in mind, I created a front garden complete with a table and chairs to greet my guests upon their arrival. I bought a dining table and placed it in a welcoming spot near a beautiful window. Then I grouped two chairs and a sofa together on a circular rug, to encourage my friends to gather. I placed this inviting conversation area in the center of my home, because sharing my home life with others was my desire and my purpose. Each room in my house became a place to invite one or more friends.

Knowing what I wanted to attract gave me a clear picture of where I needed to place my furniture and decorations. The result allowed for a meaningful gathering with my friends that matched the intentional placement in both my inner and outer home. In other words, how I set the stage in my physical home was in sync with how I wanted to live it.

The first step of the design prescription is to identify a personal goal. Look inside your center. What helps you feel good in your inner and outer home? Decorate from the sacred place within your heart. What are your core values? These are the guiding principles in your life—your

values, beliefs, and sense of purpose. Your needs help you focus and drive you toward action and achievement. Choose just one of the needs that you feel is important in your life right now. Place it with intent in your heart and mind. Consider what it means to you, how it makes you feel, and how it could help you and others in your home life.

The second part of the design prescription is to intentionally place something in your home that symbolizes your desires. Decorate your home in a way that that represents what you want in your life. Placing something in your home with intent can consciously and unconsciously remind you of what you want, every time you walk by it. For example, have you ever traveled somewhere and brought back a special item, artifact, or piece of art for your home? When you see that decoration in your home, it can instantly bring back the memory of those travels. If an object can bring to mind a fond memory, so can the intentional placement of your décor. Like a forget-me-not, that decoration can help remind you of your positive intention.

Your heart is at the center of your being. There is synergy between your feelings and values and the placement of your decorations and objects in your physical space. See with clarity and peace that you do have insight at your center to design an environment that reflects the true you. You have all the knowledge and imagination you need to create your heart-centered home!

Décor

You + Placement = Home

INTERIOROLOGY™

Prescription

Décor _____

For: _*You*_____ **Date:** _____

IP

At your center, what do you feel is one thing you need or want ?

Notes _____
_____
_____
_____

Side Effects:

This may cause you to feel inspired in your home.

INTERIOROLOGY™

Prescription

Décor

For: *Home*   **Date:** _____

IP

Intentionally place something in your home that symbolizes that need or want.

Notes _____

_____

_____

Side Effects:

This may cause your home to be intentional for you .

Chapter 7

Home Reflections

"As you live deeper in the heart, the mirror gets clearer and cleaner."
—Rumi

Home is the sacred place in our hearts where the things we love, need, and want dwell. It is the place where our only true belongings are kept. Our inner source of home is always there, and it can manifest in our living spaces, no matter where we are. Remember, by being aware of our true selves, living from our hearts, and reflecting it into our surroundings, we are able to flourish and shine. In turn, our hearts can be clarified and supported by that environment we have created, so we can continue to grow into who we want to be. From this place of alignment, we are able to inspire and serve all those on our journey through life.

After exploring the prescriptions from the last six chapters, how do you feel on the inside? How does your physical space feel? Did awareness of your internal and external worlds provide clarity, harmony, or peace in your home life?

Interiorology is a timeless guide for you to apply as your inner home resource. It is an organic system that is always expanding and changing with you. You are not alone. We are all together on an infinite path of self-discovering, transitioning through life, and connecting with our living spaces.

Be kind to yourself. Take one feeling at a time, one physical change at a time. Look for the space where you are able to connect with in your heart and home. Open your heart to knowing

yourself, and reflect that in your surroundings. Uncovering the light that is within you and expressing it in your living space is a brave choice! When you are open to who you are, you find the keys to creating your home, regardless of your current surroundings. Love, joy and serenity start at the source of you. All you need is within you: that place that feels like home.

I hope this Interiorology introduction provides you with a resource to create your authentic living space. May it help you reflect the essence of yourself and give you a place to thrive. You and the outer world are one. Know that wisdom, grace, and awareness are all within you and around you. By opening the door to your inner knower and forever feeling your way into alignment with yourself and home, the possibilities are endless!

Home Reflections

You + Environment = Home

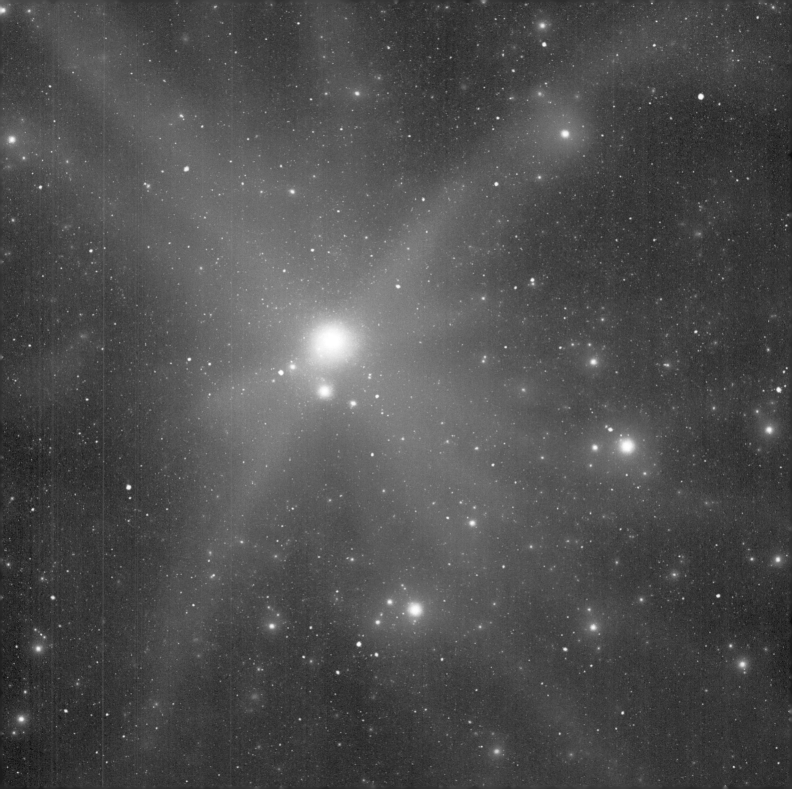

INTERIOROLOGY™

Prescription

Home Reflections

For: *You*　　　　　**Date:** _____

IP

After doing the previous prescriptions, what did you become aware of about yourself? What inspired you?

Notes _____
_____
_____
_____

Side Effects:

This may cause you to feel balanced in your home.

INTERIOROLOGY™

Prescription

Home Reflections

For: *Home*　　　　　　　**Date:** _____

IP

After doing the previous prescriptions, what did you become aware of about your home? What empowered you?

Notes _____

_____

_____

_____

Side Effects:

This may cause your home to be aligned with you.

Journals & Dreams

The next sixteen pages are spaces for you to discover and play. On the left side of the pages is a place to write about how you would like your home and you to feel. On the right side of the pages is an area for you to express yourself about those feelings. Write, draw, color, make symbols in the circle. Imagine what uplifts you, what helps you feel good and most of all have fun!

Happy home journaling and dreaming!

Feeling Clear Space

What will it feel like to have a clear space in your heart and home?
(Examples: clear, fortunate, achievement, encouraging, grounded, ease, breathe, spacious)

_____

_____

_____

_____

_____

_____

_____

_____

_____

_____

_____

_____

_____

_____

_____

_____

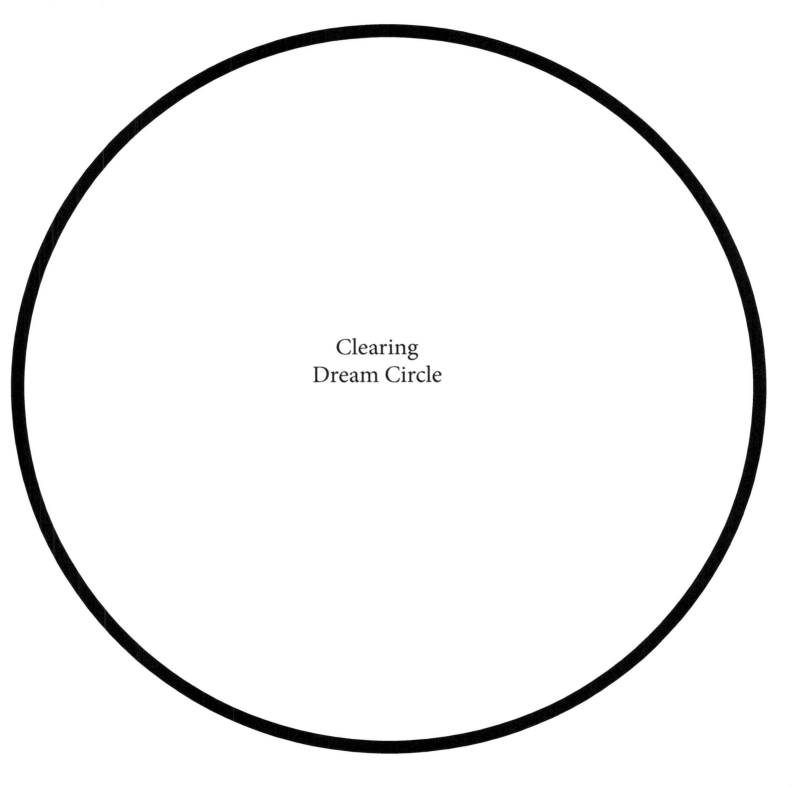

Clearing
Dream Circle

Feeling Childlike

What will it feel like to have childlike wonder in your heart and home?
(Examples: playful, enthusiasm, creativity, remembering, productive, nourishing, exploration, affectionate)

_____

_____

_____

_____

_____

_____

_____

_____

_____

_____

_____

_____

_____

_____

_____

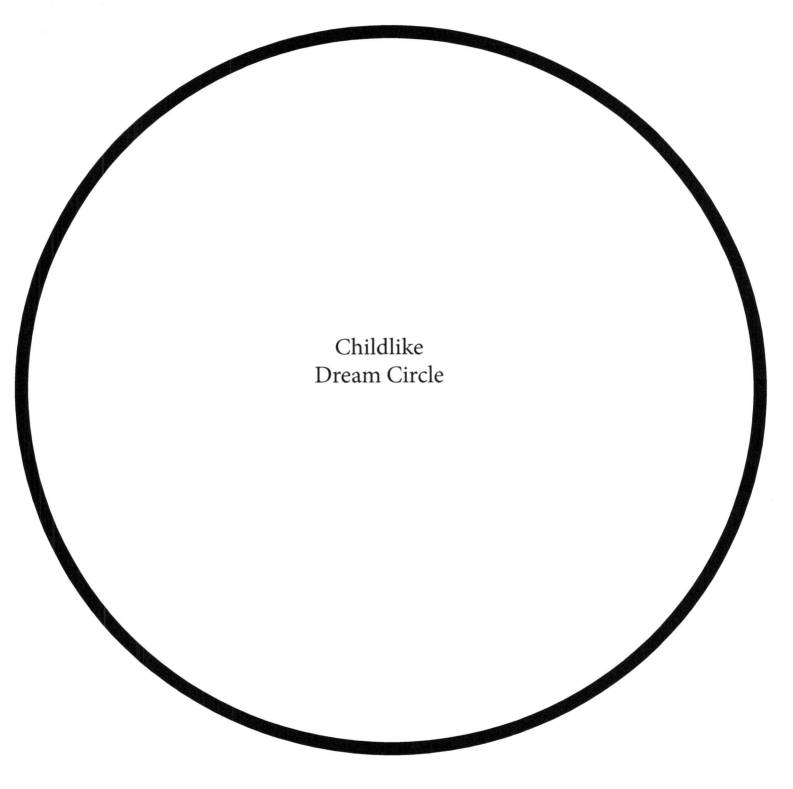

Childlike
Dream Circle

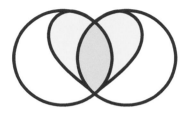

Feeling Today

What will it feel like to be aware of where you are today and going tomorrow in your heart and home?
(Examples: optimistic, self-aware, willful, luminous, insightful, energetic, joyful, present)

_____

_____

_____

_____

_____

_____

_____

_____

_____

_____

_____

_____

_____

_____

_____

_____

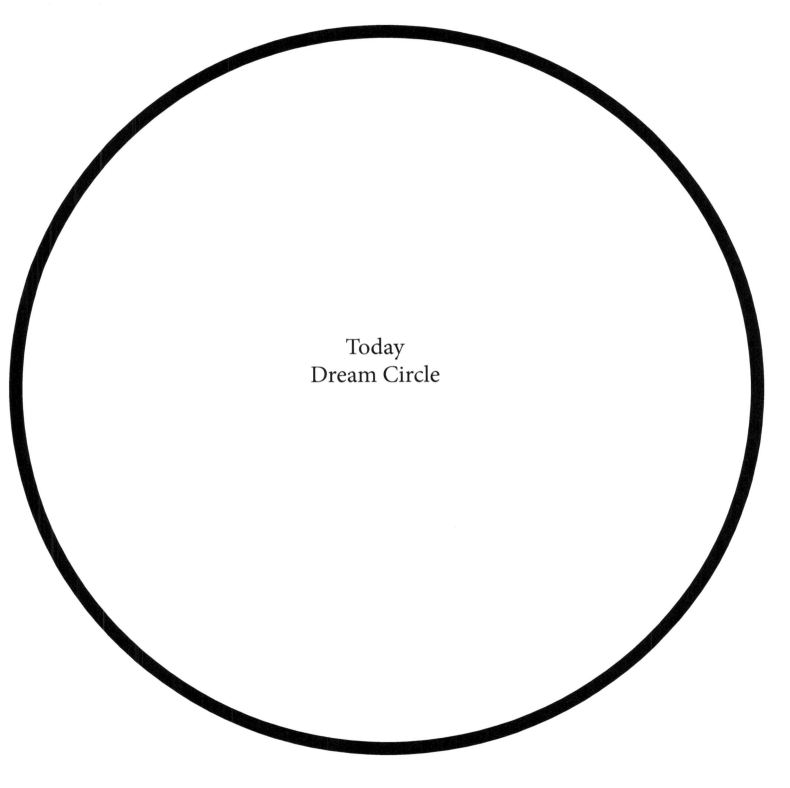

Today
Dream Circle

Feeling Nature

What will it feel like to have nature in your heart and home?
(Examples: expressive, stimulating, rhythmical, fluid, playfulness, communicative, creative, assuring)

_____
_____
_____
_____
_____
_____
_____
_____
_____
_____
_____
_____
_____
_____
_____
_____

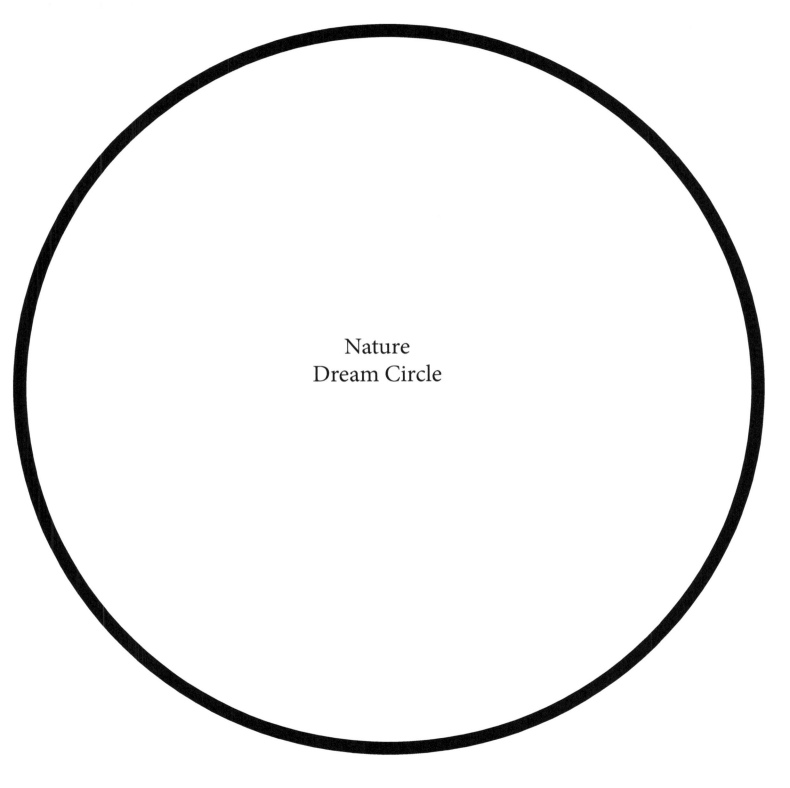

Nature
Dream Circle

Feeling Fluidity

What will it feel like to express yourself in your heart and home?
(Examples: expressive, stimulating, rhythmical, fluid, playfulness, communicative, creative, assuring)

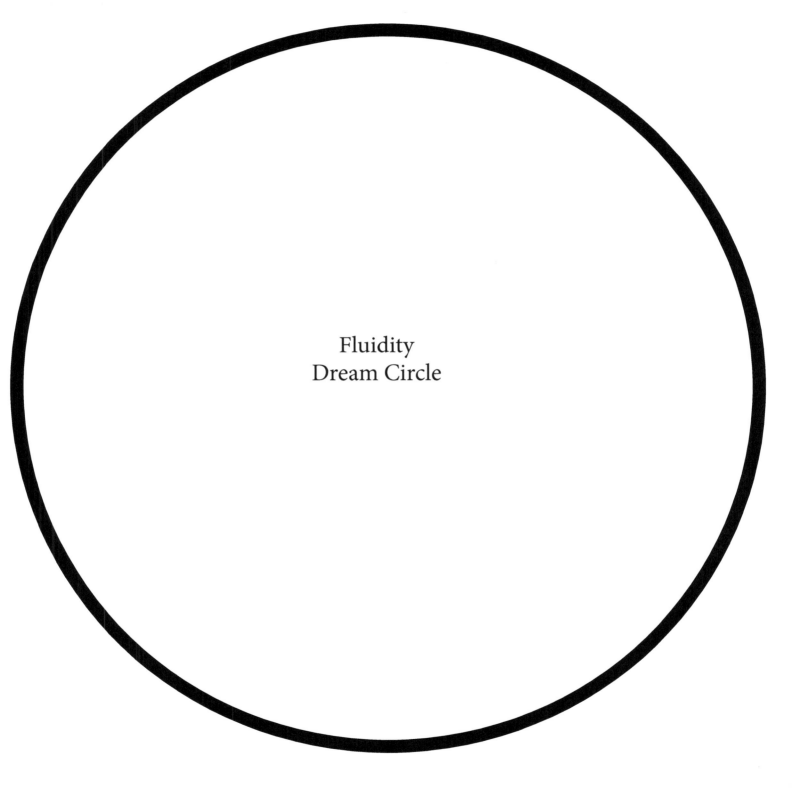

Fluidity
Dream Circle

Feeling Intentional

What will it feel like to intentionally place your ideas and artifacts in your heart and home?
(Examples: mindful, intuitive, purposeful, knowledgeable, centered, imaginative, focused, peaceful)

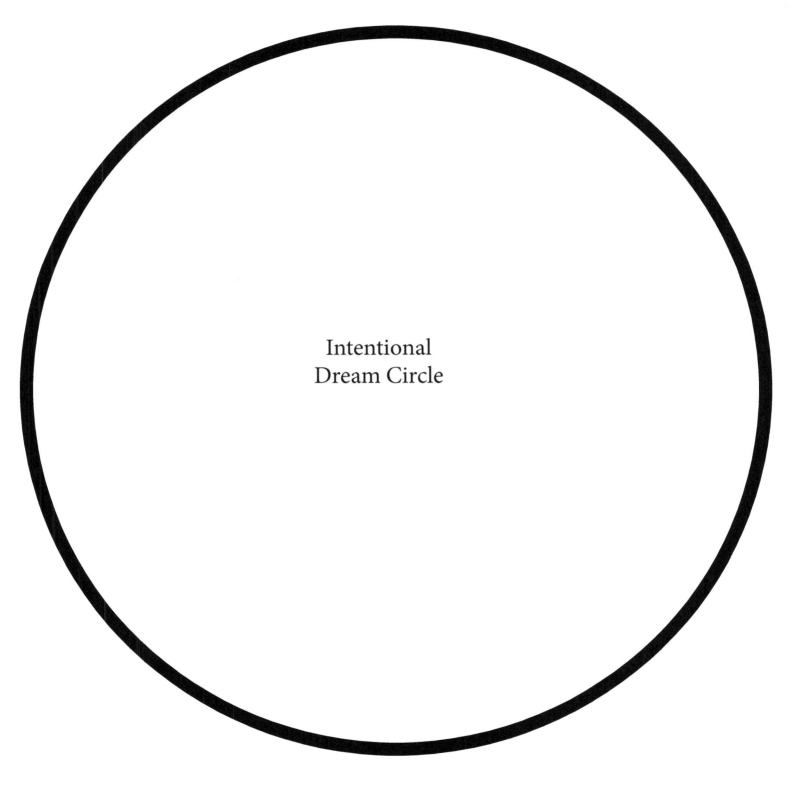

Intentional
Dream Circle

Inspiring Dream Circle

What will it feel like to be inspired in your heart and home?
(Examples: inspired, expansive, graceful, aware, synchronistic, magical, essential, authentic)

_____

_____

_____

_____

_____

_____

_____

_____

_____

_____

_____

_____

_____

_____

_____

_____

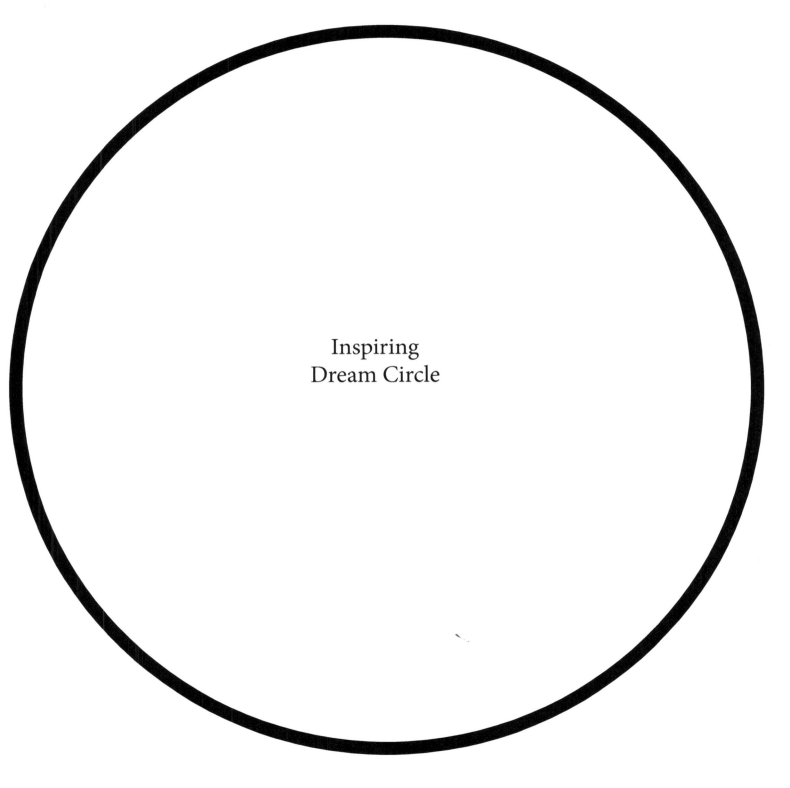

Inspiring
Dream Circle

Feeling at Home

What will it feel like to be balanced in your heart and home?

_____

_____

_____

_____

_____

_____

_____

_____

_____

_____

_____

_____

_____

_____

_____

_____

_____

_____

_____

_____

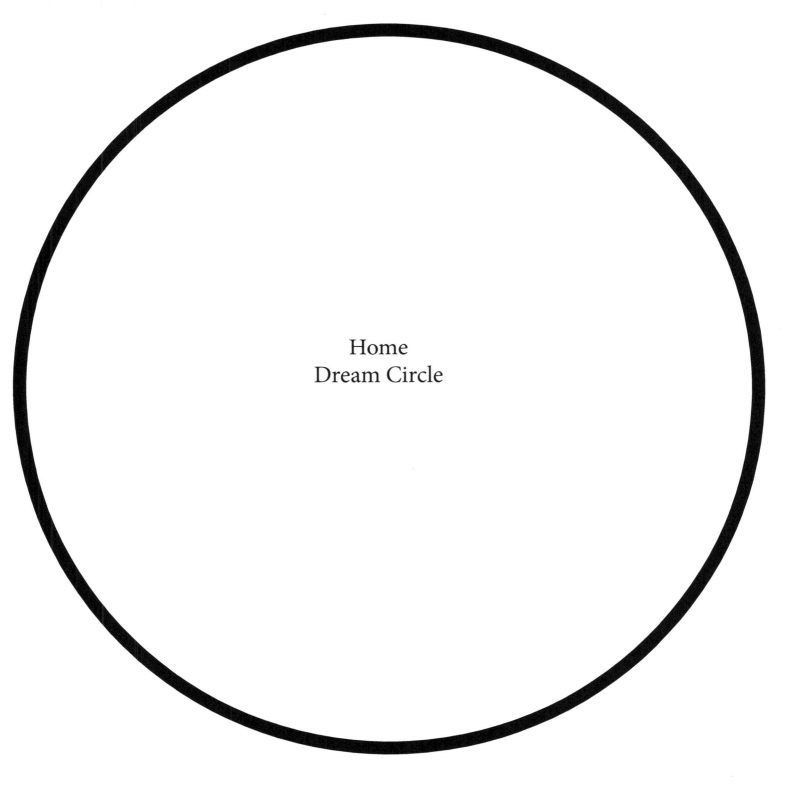

Home
Dream Circle

Dear Reader,

My hope is that you had a fun experience with this book. I wish you positive results that help you evolve in your living environment for your highest good. May it empower you to move forward with your interior surroundings for years to come!

If you are interested in learning more about Interiorology lectures, sessions and workshops, please find us at Interior-ology.com.

Smiles,

Laurel James

Bibliography

Works Cited

"Aesthetics." *Wikipedia*. Wikimedia Foundation, 24 Oct. 2012. Web. 25 Oct. 2012. <http://
  en.wikipedia.org/wiki/Aesthetics>.

Allen, James. *As A Man Thinketh*. White Plains, NY: Perer Pauper, n.d. Print.

Andrews, Mark. "How Does Background Noise Affect Our Concentration?: Scientific American."
  How Does Background Noise Affect Our Concentration?: Scientific American. Scientific American, 4
  Jan. 2010. Web. 25 Oct. 2012. <http://www.scientificamerican.com/article.cfm?id=ask-the-
  brains-background-noise>.

Augustin, Sally, PhD. *Place Advantage: Applied Psychology for Interior Architecture*. Hoboken, New Jersey:
  John Wiley & Sons, 2009. Print.

Bauhaus: The Face of the 20th Century. Dir. Frank Whitford. Perf. Fank Whitford, Charles Jencks and
  Christopher Frayling. 1994. DVD. Web.

"Bhavacakra." *Wikipedia*. Wikimedia Foundation, 22 Oct. 2012. Web. 25 Oct. 2012. <http://
  en.wikipedia.org/wiki/Bhavacakra>.

Birren, Faber. *Color Psychology And Color Therapy: A Factual Study Of The Influence Of Color On Human
  Life*. New York: University ,Inc., 1961. Print.

Booth, Mike, and Carol Mcknight. *The Aura-Soma Sourcebook: Color Therapy for the Soul*. Rochester,
  Vermont: Healing Arts, 2006. Print.

"Buckminster Fuller." *Wikipedia*. Wikimedia Foundation, n.d. Web. 25 Oct. 2012. <http://en.wikipedia.org/wiki/Buckminster_Fuller>.

Dale, Cyndi. *The Subtle Body: An Encyclopedia of Your Energetic Anatomy*. Boulder,Colorado: Sounds True, 2009. Print.

Dragowska, Urszula, Dr. TCM. "Widening the Field; A Personal Reflection on the Application of Craniosacral Biodynamic Principles in My Practice, in Health Care, and the Treatment of Cancer." N.p., n.d. Web. May 2010.

Dyer, Wayne W., Dr. *Change Your Thoughts, Change Your Life*. International: Hay House, 2007. Print.

"Ecopsychology." *Wikipedia*. Wikimedia Foundation, 23 Oct. 2012. Web. 25 Oct. 2012. <http://en.wikipedia.org/wiki/Ecopsychology>.

Elizabeth. *The Chakra Tune-up Chart*. Victoria, B.C. Canada: Onwaords & Upwords, 1992. Print.

"Environmental Psychology." *Wikipedia*. Wikimedia Foundation, 23 Oct. 2012. Web. 25 Oct. 2012. <http://en.wikipedia.org/wiki/Environmental_psychology>.

"Erik Erikson." *Wikipedia*. Wikimedia Foundation, 24 Oct. 2012. Web. 25 Oct. 2012. <http://en.wikipedia.org/wiki/Erik_Erikson>.

"Feng Shui." *Wikipedia*. Wikimedia Foundation, 22 Oct. 2012. Web. 25 Oct. 2012. <http://en.wikipedia.org/wiki/Feng_shui>.

Fox, Maxine. *Holistic Home The Homemaker's Guide to Health and Happiness*. Scotland, UK: Findhorn, 2006. Print.

Friedman, Lauren F. "Outside In: Things Are Looking Up." *Psychology Today: Health, Help, Happiness Find a Therapist*. PsychlogyToday, 01 Jan. 2011. Web. 25 Oct. 2012. <http://www.psychologytoday.com/articles/201103/outside-in-things-are-looking>.

Fritz, Robert. *The Path of Least Resistance: Principles for Creating What You Want to Create*. Salem, MA: DMA, 1984. Print.

Gaffney, Mark Aloysius. *The Psychology of the Interioro Senses*. N.p.: B. Herder Book, 1942. Print.

"Happiness." *Wikipedia*. Wikimedia Foundation, 24 Oct. 2012. Web. 25 Oct. 2012. <http://en.wikipedia.org/wiki/Happiness>.

Hawkins, David R., M.D., Ph.D. *Power vs. Force: The Hidden Determinants of Human Behavior*. International: Hay House, 2002. Print.

Hay, Louise L. *You Can Heal Your LIfe*. International: Hay House, 2004. Print.

Hemenway, Priya. *Divine Proportion: Phi In Art, Nature, and Science*. New York: Sterling, 2005. Print.

Hicks, Esther and Jerry. *Getting Into the Vortex: Guided Meditations CD and User Guide*. International: Hay House, 2010. Print.

IIardi, Stephen, Ph.D. "Social Isolation: A Modern Plague." (2009): n. pag. Psychology Today. Web. 25 Oct. 2012.

Jeffers, Susan, Ph.D. *Feel the Fear and Do It Anyway, Dynamic Techniques for Turning Fear, Indecisions, and Anger into Power,action and Love*. New York: Ballantine, 2007. Print.

Jung, C. G., and Sonu Shamdasani. *The Red Book*. New York: W.W. Norton, 2012. Print.

Klein, Sarah, and Copyright Health Magazine 2011. "To Much TV May Mean Earlier Death." *CNN*. Cable News Network, 11 Jan. 2010. Web. 25 Oct. 2012. <http://www.cnn.com/2010/HEALTH/01/11/television.tv.death/index.html>.

Lama, Dalai. *Beyond Religion Ethics for a Whole World*. New York: Houghton Mifflin Harcourt, 2011. Print.

Lennon, Robin, and Karen Plunkett Powell. *Home Design from the Inside Out: Feng Shui,Color Therapy and Self-Awareness*. New York: Penguin, 1997. Print.

Linn, Denise. *Feng Shui for the Soul: How to Create a Harmonious Environment That Will Nurture and Sustain You*. Carlsbad, CA: Hay House, 1999. Print.

Lipton, Bruce H., Ph.D. *The Biology of Belief: Unleashing the Power of Consciousness, Matter, & Miracles [.* International: Hay House, 2005. Print.

Lupton, Ellen, and J. Abbott Miller, eds. *The ABC's of Bauhaus, The Bauhaus and Design Theory.* N.p.: Princeton Architectural, n.d. Print.

Luscher, Max, Dr. *The Luscher Color Test: The Remarkable Test That Reveals Personality Through Color.* Trans. Ian A. Scott. New York, Toranto: Random House, 1969. Print.

Maddron, Tom, M.S. *Living Your Colors: Practical Wisdom for Life,Love,Work and Play.* New York: Warner, 2002. Print.

Mapes, Diane, and Msnbc.com Contributor. "Looking at Nature Makes You Nicer." *Msnbc.com.* Msnbc Digital Network, 14 Oct. 2009. Web. 25 Oct. 2012. <http://www.msnbc.msn.com/id/33243959/ns/health-behavior/t/looking-nature-makes-you-nicer/>.

Marcus, Clare Cooper, M.D., Ph.D. *House As a Mirror of Self: Exploring the Deeper Meaning of Home.* Berwick, ME: Nicolas-Hays, 2006. Print.

McDonough, William, and Michael Braungart. *Cradle To Cradle: Remaking the Way We Make Things.* New York: North Point, 2002. Print.

"Montessori Sensorial Materials." *Wikipedia.* Wikimedia Foundation, 10 Nov. 2012. Web. 25 Oct. 2012. <http://en.wikipedia.org/wiki/Montessori_sensorial_materials>.

"Myers-Briggs Type Indicator." *Wikipedia.* Wikimedia Foundation, 23 Oct. 2012. Web. 25 Oct. 2012. <http://en.wikipedia.org/wiki/Myers-Briggs_Type_Indicator>.

Myss, Caroline, Ph.D. *Anatomy of the Spirit: The Seven Stages of Power and Healing.* New York: Three River, 1996. Print.

Neville. *The Power of Awareness.* Camarilla, CA: DeVorss Publications, 1992. Print.

Nhất Hạnh, Thich Nhat. *The Heart of the Buddha's Teaching: Transforming Suffering into Peace, Joy, and Liberation.* New York: Broadway, 1999. Print.

Northrup, Christiane, M.D. *The Wisdom of Menopause Creating Physical and Emotional Health and Healing During the Change*. New York: Bantam Dell, 2006. Print.

Oz, Mehmet, Ron Arias, and Lisa Oz. *Healing from the Heart: A Leading Heart Surgeon Combines Eastern and Western Traditions to Create the Medicine of the Future*. New York: Penguin Group, 1999. Print.

Panero, Julius, and Martin Zelnik. *Human Dimension & Interior Space: A Source Book of Design Reference Standards*. London, Great Britain: Architectural, 1979. Print.

"Psychology." *Wikipedia*. Wikimedia Foundation, 22 Oct. 2012. Web. 25 Oct. 2012. <http://en.wikipedia.org/wiki/Psychology>.

Renoux, Jean. "Modern Organic Architecture from Bauhouse to Modernism." Lecture. Web. 2010. <www.iaats.com>.

Ritberger, Carol, Ph.D. *What Color Is Your Personality?: Red, Yellow, Green, Orange--*. International: Hay House, 2000. Print.

Rossbach, Sarah, and Lin Yun. *Interior Design with Feng Shui: New and Expanded*. International: Penguin Group, 2000. Print. Forward by Professor Lin Yun

Rossbach, Sarah, and Lin Yun. *Living Color: Master Lin Yuns Guide to Feng Shui and the Art of Color*. New York: Kodansha International, 1994. Print.

Roszak, Theodore, Mary E. Gomes, and Allen D. Kanner, eds. *Ecopsychology Restoring The Earth Healing The Mind*. San Francisco,CA: Sierra Club, 1995. Print. Forewords by Lester R. Brown and James Hillman

SantoPietro, Nancy. *The Anatomy of a Home: Using Feng Shui to Disarm Illness,Accelerate Recovery,and Create Optimal Health*. New York: Three Rivers, 2002. Print. Forward by H. H. Grandmaster Thomas Lin Yun Rinpoche

Saradananda, Swami. *Chakra Meditation Discover Energy, Creativity, Focus, Love, Communication, Wisdom, and Spirit*. London: Watkins, 2008. Print.

Schreiber, Katherine. "Outside In." *Get Her to the Green* March/April 2011 (n.d.): n. pag. *Psychology Today: Health, Help, Happiness Find a Therapist.* Psychology Today. Web. 25 Oct. 2012. <http://www.psychologytoday.com/collections/201203/outside-in>.

Sheehy, Gail. *Passages: Predictable Crises of Adult Life.* New York: Ballantine, 2004. Print.

Skinner, Stephen. *Sacred Geometry: Deciphering the Code.* New York: Sterling, 2006. Print.

Staff, Mayo Clinic. "Sleep Tips: 7 Steps to Better Sleep." *Mayo Clinic.* Mayo Foundation for Medical Education and Research, 07 July 2011. Web. 25 Oct. 2012. <http://www.mayoclinic.com/health/sleep/HQ01387/METHOD=print>.

Suzuki, David, Amanda Mcconnell, and Adrienne Mason. *The Sacred Balance: Rediscovering Our Place in Nature.* Vancouver, British Columbia: Greystone, 2007. Print.

Tolle, Eckhart. *A New Earth: Awakening to Your Life's Purpose.* International: Plume, Penguin, 2006. Print.

"Using Your Inner Guidance Chapter V." *New Teachings for an Awakening Humanity.* Santa Clara, CA: Spiritual Education Endeavors, n.d. N. pag. Print.

Whitehouse, Maggy. *Total Kabbalah; Bring Balance and Happiness into Your Life.* San Francisco,CA: Chronicle LLC., 2008. Print.

Winkelman, Satya, M.A, C. P. "Drawling from the inside Out-Art Playshop." Web. 2011. <http://guidetotransformation.com/>.

Laurel James lives and plays in Sarasota, Florida with her husband and blended family of three boys. She is an Interior Design graduate of Ringling School of Art and Design. Laurel is also a KRI certified Kundalini Yoga Teacher, which she considers her "Inner License". Her core principle of Interiorology started with connecting to nature as a child at her family farm in Franklin, North Carolina. Laurel's purpose is to help you thrive and find the positive aspects of your home life through introspection and delightful physical discovers.

CPSIA information can be obtained
at www.ICGtesting.com
Printed in the USA
LVHW07n0321140618
580685LV00002B/9/P